D0926890

Yo Ho Ho and
a Bottle of Rum

Acapulco

1 3/4 oz. white rum
1/2 oz. fresh lime juice
1/4 oz. triple sec
1/2 egg white
1/2 tsp. sugar
fresh mint leaves

Shake rum, lime juice, triple sec, egg white, and
sugar well with ice. Strain into a highball glass.
Garnish with mint leaves.

Bacardi Cocktail

1 1/2 oz. white or gold rum (Bacardi)
1/2 oz. lime juice
1 tsp. grenadine

Shake all ingredients well with ice.
Strain into a cocktail glass or over ice
into an old-fashioned glass.

Bahama Mama

1 1/2 oz. dark rum
1/2 oz. 151-proof rum
1/2 oz. coconut liqueur
1/2 oz. coffee liqueur
4 oz. pineapple juice
1/4 oz. lemon juice
seasonal fruit

Shake all ingredients with ice. Strain into a highball glass
filled with ice. Garnish with seasonal fruit.

Banana Daiquiri

1 ½ oz. light rum

1 tbsp. triple sec

1 ½ oz. lime juice

1 tsp. sugar

1 medium banana, sliced

Combine ingredients in a blender with 1 cup crushed ice and blend until smooth. Pour into a wineglass (or any other stemmed glass).

Beachcomber

1 1/2 oz. light rum
1/2 oz. triple sec
1/2 oz. lime juice
1 dash maraschino liqueur
lime wheel

Shake all ingredients with ice and strain into
a chilled cocktail glass with a sugared rim.
Garnish with a lime wheel.

Between the Sheets

3/4 oz. white rum

3/4 oz. brandy

1/2 oz. triple sec (ideally Cointreau)

1/2 oz. lemon juice

Shake all ingredients well with ice.

Strain into a cocktail glass.

Blue Hawaiian

1 1/2 oz. white rum
1/2 oz. blue curaçao
2 oz. pineapple juice
1 oz. coconut cream
1/2 cup crushed ice
pineapple slice
orange slice

Blend all ingredients on low speed for 10 to 15 seconds.
Pour into a large wineglass and garnish with pineapple
and orange slice.

Bolero

1 1/2 oz. white rum
3/4 oz. apple brandy
1/4 tsp. sweet vermouth
lemon twist

Stir rum, brandy, and vermouth well with ice.
Strain into a sugar-rimmed cocktail glass.
Add a twist of lemon peel as garnish.

Bolo

1 1/2 oz. white rum
1/2 oz. lemon juice
1/2 oz. orange juice
1/2 tsp. sugar
lemon slice or seasonal fruit

Shake rum, lemon and orange juice, and sugar well
with ice. Strain into a cocktail glass or sour glass.
Garnish with lemon slice or seasonal fruit.

Calypso Cooler

2 oz. white rum
3/4 oz. frozen concentrated pineapple juice, thawed
1/2 oz. lime juice
club soda
sugar to taste
pineapple slice
lime slice

Shake rum, pineapple juice, lime juice, and, if necessary, sugar well with ice. Strain into a tall highball glass filled with ice and top with cold soda. Garnish with pineapple and lime slices.

Caribbean Night

1 oz. Brugal rum

1 oz. Bacardi Limon rum

1/2 oz. passion-fruit (maracuja) juice

1 oz. mango juice

1/2 oz. lime juice

1 oz. sour mix

maraschino cherry

Shake all ingredients well with ice, strain into a cocktail glass, and garnish with a cherry.

Cuba Libre

juice of $1/2$ lime
lime twist
2 oz. light rum
cola

Put lime juice and twist of lime into a
highball glass with ice cubes, and add
rum. Fill with cola.

Daiquiri

1 ½ oz. white rum
juice of 1 lime
1 tsp. sugar

Shake all ingredients well with ice. Strain into a cocktail glass or over ice into an old-fashioned glass. Add more or less sugar, to taste.

Ernest Hemingway

1 1/2 oz. white rum
1/4 oz. maraschino
juice of 1/2 lime
1/4 oz. grapefruit juice

Shake all ingredients well with a scoop of
crushed ice . Serve in a highball glass.

Frozen Daiquiri

1 1/2 to 2 oz. white rum

1/2 oz. lime juice

1/2 to 1 tsp. sugar

1/2 cup crushed ice

Put all ingredients into a blender.

Blend at low speed for 10 to 15 seconds.

Pour into a chilled cocktail glass.

Gauguin

2 oz. white rum
1/2 oz. passion-fruit syrup
1/2 oz. lemon juice
1/4 oz. lime juice
1/3 cup crushed ice
maraschino cherry

Blend rum, passion-fruit syrup, lemon and lime juice,
and ice at low speed for 10 to 15 seconds. Pour into
a large, chilled cocktail glass and add cherry.

Havana Sidecar

1 1/2 oz. gold rum
3/4 oz. triple sec
3/4 oz. lemon juice

Shake all ingredients well over
ice. Strain into a chilled
cocktail glass.

Honolulu Juicer

1 1/2 oz. Southern Comfort
3/4 oz. dark rum
2 oz. pineapple juice
3/4 oz. lemon juice
3/4 oz. Rose's lime juice
1 small tsp. powdered sugar
pineapple slice

Shake all ingredients over ice. Strain into a large highball
glass over ice and garnish with pineapple.

Hurricane

1 oz. dark rum

1 oz. light rum

1 tbsp. passion-fruit syrup

2 tsp. lime juice

lime wedge

1/2 oz. orange juice (optional)

1/2 oz. pineapple juice (optional)

Shake all ingredients with ice and strain into a
highball glass over crushed ice; garnish with a
lime wedge. For a fruitier drink, add equal
parts orange juice and pineapple juice.

Jamaica Rum Cocktail

1 1/2 oz. dark rum
3/4 oz. lime juice
1 tsp. sugar
lime wedge

Shake all ingredients well with ice. Strain into a cocktail glass. Garnish with a lime wedge.

Mai Tai

2 oz. light rum

1 oz. triple sec

1 tbsp. orgeat (or almond-flavored syrup)

1 tbsp. grenadine

1 tbsp. lime juice

$1/2$ tsp. powdered sugar

pineapple wedge

maraschino cherry

dash of high-proof dark rum (optional)

Shake all ingredients with ice and strain into a large old-fashioned glass about 1/3 full with crushed ice. Decorate with a cherry speared to a wedge of fresh pineapple. Serve with straws. For a Mai Tai with more kick, try topping the drink with a dash of high-proof dark rum.

Mango Daiquiri

1 1/2 oz. light rum
1 tbsp. triple sec
1 1/2 oz. lime juice
1 tsp. sugar
2 oz. pureed mango

Combine ingredients in a blender with 1 cup crushed
ice and blend until smooth. Pour into a wineglass
(or any other stemmed glass).

Mojito

1/2 tsp. powdered sugar

juice of 1/2 lime

2 oz. white rum

club soda

mint leaves

Stir sugar and lime juice well in a large highball glass. Crush in mint leaves with a pestle, add the squeezed half lime. Fill with crushed ice, add rum, stir. Add soda to fill glass, and garnish with a mint sprig.

Mulatta

1 ³/₄ oz. white rum
¹/₄ oz. brown crème de cacao
juice of ¹/₂ lime

Mix ingredients in a
blender with a scoop of
crushed ice. Serve in an
iced cocktail glass.

Patria Colada

1 oz. passion-fruit (maracuja) juice
 (concentrated, not diluted)
1 oz. coconut milk
1 oz. Myer's rum
coconut
mango

Place passion-fruit juice and coconut milk in a blender
with two cups of crushed ice. Blend at high speed for a
short time. Pour into a highball glass and float rum on
top. Garnish with shaved coconut and chopped mango.

Piña Colada

3 oz. light rum
3 tbsp. coconut milk
3 tbsp. crushed pineapple or 3 oz. pineapple juice

Place ingredients in a blender with two cups of crushed ice. Blend at high speed for a short time or mix in a shaker with crushed ice. Strain into a highball glass and serve with a straw. Pineapple juice can be substituted for the crushed pineapple, using equal parts rum and juice.

Planter's Punch

juice of 2 limes

2 tsp. powdered sugar

2 oz. club soda

2 1/2 oz. light or dark rum

2 dashes bitters

1 dash grenadine

lemon slice

orange slice

pineapple slice

stemmed maraschino cherry

Mix first three ingredients in a highball glass, add ice cubes, and stir until glass is frosted. Add rum and bitters. Stir and top with grenadine. Decorate with fruit.

Rum Citrus Cooler

2 oz. white rum
1/2 oz. triple sec
1 oz. orange juice
1/2 oz. fresh lime juice
1 tsp. sugar
lemon-lime soda (e.g., 7-Up)
lemon wedge
lime wedge

Shake all but soda well with ice. Strain over ice into a highball glass. Fill drink with soda and stir. Garnish with lemon and lime wedges.

Rum Fizz

2 oz. white rum
3/4 oz. lemon juice
1/2 oz. sugar syrup*
club soda

Shake first three ingredients over ice and strain
into a highball glass over ice. Fill with soda.

*To make 16 oz. sugar syrup, slowly dissolve 1 lb.
granulated sugar in 13 oz. hot water.

Rum Highball

2 oz. white or dark rum
ginger ale, 7-Up, or tonic water
lemon peel

Pour rum into a highball glass over ice, fill with
soda or tonic, and garnish with lemon peel.

Rum Punch

1 oz. dark rum

1 oz. white rum

1 oz. gold rum

2 oz. orange juice

2 oz. pineapple juice

juice of 1/2 lime

1 dash grenadine

lemon slice

orange slice

pineapple slice

stemmed maraschino cherry

Shake rum and juices with ice and pour into a tall highball glass. Top with grenadine. Decorate with fruit.

Rum Rickey

1 ½ oz. light rum
½ small lime
club soda

Add rum to a highball glass with ample ice. Squeeze lime over the drink before dropping it into the glass. Fill with soda and stir.

Santiago

1 1/2 oz. white rum

juice of 1 lime

1/4 oz. grenadine

sugar to taste

lime peel

Shake all ingredients well with ice. Strain into a
cocktail glass. Garnish with lime peel.

Scorpion

1 oz. dark rum

3/4 oz. white rum

3/4 oz. brandy

1/4 oz. triple sec

1 1/2 oz. orange juice

juice of 1/2 lime

Shake all ingredients well over crushed ice, strain into a large highball glass half-filled with crushed ice, and drop the squeezed lime into the glass before serving.

South Sea

1 1/2 oz. white rum
3/4 oz. curaçao
3/4 oz. lime juice

Shake all ingredients well with ice.
Strain into a cocktail glass.

West Indian Punch

2 oz. dark rum
3/4 oz. banana liqueur
1 oz. pineapple juice
1 oz. orange juice
juice of 1/2 lime
nutmeg

Shake all ingredients over ice, strain into a highball glass
over ice, and sprinkle with nutmeg.

Yellow Bird

1 oz. dark rum

1 oz. white rum

1/4 oz. Tia Maria

1 1/4 oz. orange juice

juice of 1/2 lime

stemmed maraschino cherry

mint leaves

Shake all ingredients over ice. Strain into a large highball glass over ice. Garnish with cherry and mint leaves.

Zombie

2 oz. dark rum

3/4 oz. light rum

1/2 oz. high-proof dark rum

3/4 oz. cherry brandy

1 1/4 oz. lemon juice

3/4 oz. blood-orange juice

3 dashes grenadine

pineapple stick, maraschino cherry, or mint leaves

Combine all ingredients well over ice cubes in a shaker.
Strain into a large highball glass half-filled with crushed ice.
The drink can be garnished with a stick of pineapple, a
cherry, or a sprig of fresh mint dipped in powdered sugar.

Welcome to Margaritaville: Tequila and Other Pleasures

Blue Margarita

1 1/2 oz. tequila
1/2 oz. blue curaçao
1/2 oz. triple sec
1 oz. lemon or lime juice
lemon or lime rind

Rub rim of a cocktail glass with lemon or lime rind
and dip rim in salt. Shake all ingredients with ice and
strain into the salt-rimmed glass.

Cactus Pear Margarita

1 1/2 oz. white tequila

1/2 oz. triple sec

1 1/2 oz. fresh lime juice

2 oz. cactus pear puree*

lime wheel

lemon twist

Shake tequila, triple sec, lime juice, and cactus pear puree well with ice. Strain into a sugar-rimmed cocktail glass. Garnish with lime wheel and lemon twist.

*Puree fruit in a blender. Add 1 tsp. of sugar, or more if needed. Strain and discard seeds. One fruit will yield approximately 4 oz. puree.

Caipirinha

2 tsp. granulated sugar
1 lime, cut into 8 wedges
2 1/2 oz. cachaça

Mash the sugar and lime in an old-fashioned glass. Pour the cachaça into the glass and stir well. Fill the glass with ice cubes or crushed ice and stir again.

Cherimoya Coconut Tequila

1 1/2 oz. white tequila

1/4 oz. cream of coconut

1/2 oz. fresh lemon juice

3 oz. cherimoya puree*

1/2 cup crushed ice

cinnamon stick

Put all ingredients except cinnamon stick into a blender and blend 20 seconds at low speed. Pour into a large, chilled cocktail glass. Garnish with cinnamon stick.

*Mash fruit through a strainer. Discard the seeds. Add a pinch of ground cinnamon and 1/2 tbsp. sugar, or more if needed. One fruit will yield approximately 3 oz. puree.

Ginger-Coconut Margarita (Gingerita)

1 1/2 oz. tequila
1/2 oz. triple sec
1 oz. lime juice
1 oz. sour mix
1 oz. coconut cream
1 oz. Canton ginger liqueur
lime wheel
powdered ginger

Put all ingredients in a blender and blend 20 seconds at low speed. Pour into a chilled cocktail glass. Garnish with a lime wheel covered in ginger.

Margarita

1 1/2 oz. tequila
1/2 oz. triple sec
1 oz. lemon or lime juice
lemon or lime rind

Rub rim of a cocktail glass with lemon or lime rind and dip rim in salt. Shake all ingredients with ice and strain into the salt-rimmed cocktail glass.

Pisco Sour

1 1/2 oz. Pisco brandy
juice of 1/2 lemon
1/2 to 1 tsp. powdered sugar, to taste
stemmed maraschino cherry

Shake ingredients well over ice cubes
in a shaker, strain into a sour glass, and
garnish with a cherry.

Pisco Sour,
Peruvian Style

1 1/2 to 2 oz. Pisco brandy

1 oz. lime juice

1 oz. sour mix

1 tsp. powdered sugar

1 egg white

dashes bitters

lime wheel

Shake all except bitters well with ice and strain into sour glass. Top with bitters and garnish with a lime wheel. This also can be made by putting all the ingredients in a blender and adding a few cubes of ice, to make a more full-bodied drink.

Sangria

4 tbsp. sugar

1 cup water

1 bottle (750 ml) red wine

1 orange, thinly sliced

1 lime, thinly sliced

other fruit, such as strawberries, bananas, etc.

$\frac{1}{2}$ cup club soda or sparkling water

Dissolve sugar in water in large pitcher. Add wine, fruit, and ice. Stir until cold. Add soda or bubbly water before pouring into large wineglasses, making sure that each glass gets some fruit. Serves eight.

Tequila Sunrise

lime wedge

2 oz. tequila

4 oz. orange juice

$^3/_4$ oz. grenadine

Squeeze lime into a large highball glass half-filled with
ice and drop it into the glass. Stir tequila and orange
juice with ice and strain into the glass. Pour grenadine in
slowly and allow to settle. Stir to make the sunrise.

From Martinis to Bikinis: Gin and Vodka Go to the Beach

Curaçao Cooler

1 oz. vodka
1 oz. blue curaçao
$1/2$ oz. lime juice
$1/2$ oz. lemon juice
orange juice
lemon peel
lime peel
orange peel

Shake all but orange juice well with ice. Strain into a tall highball glass filled with ice and top with well-chilled orange juice. Garnish with lemon, lime, and orange peels.

Gimlet

1 oz. lime juice
1 1/2 oz. gin

Shake well with ice and strain into a cocktail glass.
Powdered sugar may be added, to taste.

Gin Fizz

juice of ½ lemon
1 tsp. powdered sugar
2 oz. gin
club soda

Shake first three ingredients with ice and
strain into a highball glass with a few ice
cubes. Fill with soda and stir.

Gin Rickey

1 1/2 oz. gin
juice of 1/2 lime
club soda
lime wedge

Combine gin and lime juice in a highball glass with ice
cubes. Fill with soda and stir. Garnish with a wedge of
lime before serving.

Gin and Tonic

lime

2 oz. gin

tonic water

Squeeze lime over ice cubes
in a highball glass, add gin,
and fill with tonic. Stir.

Long Island Iced Tea

1/2 oz. vodka

1/2 oz. gin

1/2 oz. light rum

1/2 oz. tequila

juice of 1/2 lemon

1 dash cola

lemon slice

Combine ingredients and pour over ice into a highball glass. Add cola for color. Garnish with a slice of lemon.

Madras

1 1/2 oz. vodka

4 oz. cranberry juice

1 oz. orange juice

lime wedge

Pour all ingredients into a highball glass over
ice and stir. Garnish with a wedge of lime.

Paradise

1 1/2 oz. gin
1/2 oz. apricot brandy
1 oz. orange juice

Shake all ingredients well with ice.
Strain into a cocktail glass.

Salty Dog

1 1/2 oz. vodka or 1 1/2 oz. gin
3 1/2 oz. grapefruit juice
salt

Shake vodka and juice with ice in a shaker and pour
into a chilled cocktail glass rimmed with salt. A pinch
of salt may also be added to the drink. Gin may be
substituted for the vodka, using a greater amount of
juice, to taste.

Seabreeze

1 1/2 oz. vodka
4 oz. cranberry juice
1 oz. grapefruit juice
lime wedge

Pour all ingredients into a highball glass over ice cubes.
Stir, and garnish with a wedge of lime.

Singapore Sling

2 oz. gin
juice of 1/2 lemon
1 tsp. powdered sugar
club soda
1/2 oz. cherry-flavored brandy
seasonal fruit

Shake gin, lemon juice, and sugar with ice and strain into a highball glass. Add ice cubes and fill with soda. Float cherry-flavored brandy on top. Decorate with fruits in season and serve with a straw.

Southside

1 1/2 oz. gin
1 tsp. powdered sugar
juice of 1/2 lemon
mint leaves

Shake gin, sugar, and lemon juice with ice
and strain into a chilled cocktail glass.
Garnish with two sprigs of fresh mint.

Vodka Stinger

1 oz. vodka
1 oz. crème de menthe (white)
mint leaves (optional)

Shake ingredients with ice and
strain into a chilled cocktail
glass. Garnish with mint leaves,
if desired.

Tropical
Cocktail
Timeline

7th Century B.C.
Greek symposium (and social drinking) initiated.

478 B.C.
Confucius warns against drunkenness.

14th Century A.D.
First mixed drink, the Bragget, concocted by combining mead and ale.

1720
So-called Gin Epidemic begins in London.

1736
Britain passes the Gin Act to limit gin production.

1742
Gin Act repealed.

22 March 1773
Chemist Joseph Priestly invents carbonated water.

1784
Benjamin Rush, "father of the temperance movement," publishes *An Inquiry into the Effects of Ardent Spirits*

upon the Human Minde and Body.

13 May 1806
First known use in print of the word *cocktail*, attributed to the American periodical *The Balance*.

1 May 1851
Opening of the first cocktail bar, at Gore House near Hyde Park, London.

4 October 1851
First cocktail bar closes. License not renewed.

1862
Infamous barman "Professor" Jerry Thomas publishes first cocktail book, *The Bar-Tender's Guide* (also known as *The Bon Vivant's Guide*, or *How to Mix Drinks*).

1915
Singapore Sling created at Raffles Hotel bar by legendary bartender Ngiam Tong Boon to suit the tastes of visitors from the West.

16 January 1920
Prohibition becomes law in the United States.

26 April 1924
British writer Alec Waugh (brother of author Evelyn) throws "first" cocktail party.

5 December 1933
Prohibition repealed.

12 May 1935
Alcoholics Anonymous founded by William Wilson ("Bill W").

1939
So-called Cocktail Age ends. Germany invades Poland.

1944
The Mai Tai invented in Oakland by Californian Victor "Trader Vic" Bergeron, who also concocts the Fog Cutter, Scorpion, and others.

1945
The Lost Weekend is released.

1947
Under the Volcano, Malcolm Lowry's paean to mescal, is published.

Glassware and
Bar Equipment

Glassware

The long and short of glassware is: size matters.
Have a variety of sizes.

Cocktail Glass
A stemmed glass with a rounded bowl.

Highball, or Collins Glass
A large, multipurpose cocktail glass. For everything
from a Gin Fizz to a Long Island Iced Tea. Holds
between eight and twelve ounces.

Old-Fashioned Glass
The stout, sturdy tumbler. Perfect for a Caipirinha.
Contains between six and ten ounces.

Sour Glass
A narrow, stemmed glass perfectly proportioned for sours of four to seven ounces.

Wineglass
Useful for cream drinks and punches, and in a pinch can fill in for just about any drink.

That is the basic lineup. Of course, many more could be on hand for specialty drinks. And don't forget the paper parasols.

Bar Equipment

The list of "necessary" equipment and glassware in most bartender's guides is nearly enough to put one off the notion of mixing drinks. Here, however, are some key components to have behind the bar:

Can Opener

Jigger

The best one is two-sided: the larger cup holds either two ounces or one and a half ounces; the smaller side holds either one ounce or three quarters of an ounce.

Juicer

The difference between fresh-squeezed juice and store-bought varieties can be enormous—maybe not with a Screwdriver, but certainly with a Margarita. An old-fashioned juicer with a bowl is sufficient.

Long Spoon, or Stirrer

Let's face it, anything that is clean and can reach the bottom of the mixing glass will suffice.

Paring Knife and Cutting Board

Neither need be elaborate. A sharp blade is essential. The board does not have to be large; you will be most often cutting lime wedges or trimming peels for a twist.

Shaker

The fundamental item. It should be large enough to handle two full drinks and ice, approximately 14 ounces. The Boston shaker is a popular model. It pairs one tall glass with a slightly larger steel container. Another favorite shaker is the stainless steel variety that comes with a strainer built into the lid and a cap roughly the size of a two-ounce jigger. This style of shaker conveniently eliminates two pieces of equipment generally considered required: the strainer and the jigger/shot glass.

Strainer

A piece of ice ruins a neat drink. If you opt for a shaker that cannot perform the task of straining, get a Hawthorn strainer, the type with the coil spring around its head to keep it snug. It is functional and has a certain amount of retro-chic.

Waiter's Corkscrew

Ideal because it folds up like a pocket knife and includes a standard bottle opener, too.

Glossary

Angostura Bitters

Best-selling brand of bitters, named after a town in Venezuela where a physician from Germany made it to combat malaria. Consists of an extract from the bark of the Casparia tree, plus herbs and spices.

Cointreau

White French liqueur flavored with the peel of sour and other oranges.

Curaçao

Orange-flavored liqueur originally produced in Holland from sour oranges, cane sugar, and brandy.

Fifth

Seven hundred fifty milliliters, or approximately 25.4 ounces; about a fifth of a gallon.

Fizz

Drink with carbonated water that is shaken before serving, ideally with the glass foaming at the brim.

Float

A minute portion of liquor poured gently on top of a drink.

Highball

Any tall drink over ice with plain or carbonated water, always without juice.

Neat

Describes a drink served without ice.

Rose's lime juice

Best-known brand, which allegedly predates the drink most closely associated with it, the Gimlet. First made by Lauchlin Rose of Scotland in 1867, sold to shipping companies to relieve scurvy among sailors.

Sling

Mix of lemon and sugar or sweet liqueur.

Sour

A drink of liquor, lemon juice, and sugar (and some-
times a bit of orange juice, too).

Triple Sec

A liqueur made from citrus fruits; Cointreau is the best-
known variety of triple sec.

Twist

A small slice of citrus peel, squeezed over a drink (and,
on occasion, rubbed around the rim of the glass).

Selected Bibliography

Babor, Thomas, Ph.D. *Alcohol: Customs and Rituals.*
New York: Chelsea House, 1986.
  A volume of the Encyclopedia of Psychoactive Drugs.
  Histories and comparative studies of drinking in differ-
  ent countries.

Barr, Andrew. *Drink.* New York: Bantam, 1995.
  An enthusiastic look at historic and contemporary con-
  sumption of alcohol in Great Britain, for the most part.

Cotton, Leo, edited by Susan Suffes. *Mr. Boston: Official Bartender's and Party Guide.* New York: Warner Books, 1994.
  The old bible of cocktails. Authoritative, given its
  more than sixty editions since 1935. Complete with bar
  tricks.

Dunkling, Leslie. *The Guinness Drinking Companion.*
London: Guinness Publishing, 1992.
  Surprisingly nonregional and an excellent source of
  literary references to drink.

Gay, Kathlyn, and Martin Gay. *Encyclopedia of North American Eating & Drinking Traditions, Customs & Rituals*. Santa Barbara, Calif.: ABC-Clio, 1996.
    More about eating than drinking.

Jackson, Michael. *Michael Jackson's Cocktail Book*. London: Mitchell Beazley, 1994.
    Well-illustrated book from the author of the better-known *World Guide to Whisky* and *Pocket Bartender's Guide*.

Regan, Gary. *The Bartender's Bible*. New York: HarperCollins, 1991.
    One thousand and one mixed drinks in a handy, lie-flat, spiral-bound book.

Schumann, Charles. *American Bar*. New York: Abbeville Press, 1995.
    The new bible of cocktails. Handsome, informative, if surprisingly sober.

———. *Tropical Bar Book: Drinks and Stories*. New York: Stewart, Tabori and Chang, 1989.
    A walk on the wilder side, mixing drinks and bibulous prose.

Indexes

Index of Drink Names

Page numbers in *italic* indicate a recipe accompanied by a photograph

Acapulco, *22*
Bacardi Cocktail, *25*
Bahama Mama, *26*
Banana Daiquiri, *28*
Beachcomber, *31*
Between the Sheets, *33*
Blue Hawaiian, 8, *34*
Blue Margarita, *103*
Bolero, *37*
Bolo, *39*
Cactus Pear Margarita, *104*
Caipirinha, 13, *107*, 160
Calypso Cooler, *40*
Caribbean Night, *42*
Cherimoya Coconut Tequila, *108*
Cuba Libre, *45*
Curaçao Cooler, *127*

Daiquiri, 10, *46*. *See also* Banana Daiquiri; Bolo; Frozen Daiquiri; Jamaica Rum Cocktail; Mango Daiquiri
Ernest Hemingway, *49*
Frozen Daiquiri, *50*
Gauguin, *53*
Gimlet, *129*, 170
Gin and Tonic, *134*
Gin Fizz, *131*, 160
Ginger-Coconut Margarita (Gingerita), *111*
Gin Rickey, *132*
Havana Sidecar, *55*
Honolulu Juicer, *56*
Hurricane, *58*
Jamaica Rum Cocktail, *61*
Long Island Iced Tea, *136*, 160

Madras, *139*
Mai Tai, *8-9, 10, 62, 156*
Mango Daiquiri, *65*
Margarita, *16-17, 114, 163.*
    See also Blue Margarita;
    Cactus Pear Margarita;
    Ginger-Coconut Margarita
Mojito, *67*
Mulatta, *68*
Paradise, *140*
Patria Colada, *73*
Piña Colada, *10, 74*
Pisco Sour, *117*
Pisco Sour, Peruvian Style, *118*
Planter's Punch, *77*
Rum Citrus Cooler, *78*
Rum Fizz, *81*
Rum Highball, *82*
Rum Punch, *85*
Rum Rickey, *87*
Salty Dog, *143*

Sangria, *121*
Santiago, *88*
Scorpion, *90, 156*
Seabreeze, *144*
Singapore Sling, *146, 155*
South Sea, *93*
Southside, *149*
Tequila Sunrise, *122*
Vodka Stinger, *151*
West Indian Punch, *94*
Yellow Bird, *97*
Zombie, *8, 10, 98*

Index of Ingredients

Page numbers in *italic* indicate a recipe accompanied by a
   photograph

Brandy
Between the Sheets, *33*
Scorpion, *90*, 156

APPLE
Bolero, *37*

APRICOT
Paradise, *140*

CHERRY
Zombie, 8, 10, 98
Singapore Sling, *146*, 155

PISCO
Pisco Sour, *117*
Pisco Sour, Peruvian Style, *118*

Cachaça
Caipirinha, *13*, *107*, 160

Coconut
Bahama Mama (coconut
   liqueur), 26
Blue Hawaiian (coconut cream),
   8, *34*
Patria Colada (coconut milk), *73*
Piña Colada (coconut milk), 74
Cherimoya Coconut Tequila
   (coconut cream), *108*
Ginger-Coconut Margarita (Gin-
   gerita) (coconut cream), *111*

Curaçao, 169
South Sea, 93

   BLUE CURAÇAO
   Blue Hawaiian, 8, *34*
   Blue Margarita, *103*
   Curaçao Cooler, *127*

Gin
Gimlet, *129*, 170
Gin Fizz, *131*, 160
Gin Rickey, *132*
Gin and Tonic, *134*
Long Island Iced Tea, *136*, 160
Paradise, *140*
Salty Dog, *143*
Singapore Sling, *146*, 155
Southside, *149*

Rum, 9–13

   DARK RUM
   Bahama Mama, *26*
   Honolulu Juicer, *56*
   Hurricane, *58*
   Jamaica Rum Cocktail, *61*
   Planter's Punch, *77*
   Rum Highball, *82*
   Rum Punch, *85*
   Scorpion, *90*, 156
   West Indian Punch, *94*
   Yellow Bird, *97*
   Zombie, 8, 10, *98*

   GOLD RUM
   Bacardi Cocktail, *25*
   Havana Sidecar, *55*
   Patria Colada (Myers's rum),
      73
   Rum Punch, *85*

HIGH-PROOF RUM

Bahama Mama, *26*
Zombie, *8, 10, 98*

WHITE/LIGHT RUM

Acapulco, *22*
Bacardi Cocktail, *25*
Banana Daiquiri, *28*
Beachcomber, *31*
Between the Sheets, *33*
Blue Hawaiian, *8, 34*
Bolero, *37*
Bolo, *39*
Calypso Cooler, *40*
Caribbean Night (Bacardi Limon rum), *42*
Cuba Libre, *45*
Daiquiri, *10, 46*
Ernest Hemingway, *49*
Frozen Daiquiri, *50*

Gauguin, *53*
Hurricane, *58*
Long Island Iced Tea, *136, 160*
Mai Tai, *8–9, 10, 62, 156*
Mango Daiquiri, *65*
Mojito, *67*
Mulatta, *68*
Piña Colada, *10, 74*
Planter's Punch, *77*
Rum Citrus Cooler, *78*
Rum Fizz, *81*
Rum Highball, *82*
Rum Punch, *85*
Rum Rickey, *87*
Santiago, *88*
Scorpion, *90, 156*
South Sea, *93*
Yellow Bird, *97*
Zombie, *8, 10, 98*

Tequila, 14–17

Blue Margarita, *103*
Cactus Pear Margarita, *104*
Cherimoya Coconut Tequila, *108*
Ginger-Coconut Margarita
 (Gingerita), *111*
Long Island Iced Tea, *136*, *160*
Margarita, 16–17, *114*, *163*
Tequila Sunrise, *122*

Vodka

Curaçao Cooler, *127*
Long Island Iced Tea, *136*, *160*
Madras, *139*
Salty Dog, *143*
Seabreeze, *144*
Vodka Stinger, *151*

Wine

Sangria, *121*

Index of Drink Types

Page numbers in *italic* indicate a recipe accompanied by a
  photograph

Coladas
Patria Colada, *73*
Piña Colada, 10, *74*

Coolers
Calypso Cooler, *40*
Curaçao Cooler, *127*
Rum Citrus Cooler, *78*
Rum Highball, *82*

Daiquiris
Bolo, *39*
Banana Daiquiri, *28*
Daiquiri, 10, *46*
Frozen Daiquiri, *50*
Jamaica Rum Cocktail, *61*
Mango Daiquiri, *65*

Fizzes
Gin Fizz, *131*, *160*
Rum Fizz, *81*

Frozen
Banana Daiquiri, *28*
Blue Hawaiian, 8, *34*
Cherimoya Coconut Tequila,
    108
Frozen Daiquiri, *50*
Gauguin, *53*
Mango Daiquiri, *65*
Patria Colada, *73*
Piña Colada, 10, *74*

Margaritas
Blue Margarita, *103*
Cactus Pear Margarita, *104*
Ginger-Coconut Margarita (Gingerita), *111*
Margarita, 16-17, *114, 163*

Punches
Planter's Punch, *77*
Rum Punch, *85*
Sangria, *121*
West Indian Punch, *94*

Rickeys
Gin Rickey, *132*
Rum Rickey, *87*

Sours
Pisco Sour, *117*
Pisco Sour, Peruvian Style, *118*
Southside, *149*

Photography Credits

Front cover, back cover, spine detail, title page detail, and frontispiece: Photograph by Kenneth Chen, New York/Copyright © Abbeville Press.

Photograph by Mary Ellen Bartley, New York/Copyright © Abbeville Press: 26, 28, 99, 102, 137, 142, 150; Ward Beckett: 165; Photograph by Kenneth Chen, New York/Copyright © Abbeville Press: 20–21, 23–24, 27, 35–36, 38, 41, 43, 47–48, 51–52, 54, 57, 60, 64–66, 69, 72, 75–76, 79–80, 83–84, 86, 89, 91–92, 95–96, 100–102, 105, 108, 110, 115, 119–20, 124–26, 132, 135, 140–41, 145; Copyright © Tony Cenicola: 106; Photograph by Steve Cohen, New York/Copyright © Abbeville Press: 138, 148; Louis Dormand: 174–75; Copyright © Larry Dunmire/Photo Network, Tustin, Calif.: 147; Fischgrund: 15; Copyright © Fotohandel Sunny Isle, L. Reck, Curaçao: 168, 184; Foto Mexicana: 171; Lito Juventud: 190; H. W. Hannau: 166–67; F. S. Lincoln, Corinthian Publications, Inc., New York: 152–53; Copyright © Fred Lyon, San Francisco: 63; Luis Márquez: 157, 162; Photograph by Judd Pilossof, New York/Copyright © Abbeville Press: 116; Photograph by Alan Richardson, New York/Copyright © Abbeville Press: 130; Mike Roberts, Color Productions, Berkeley, Calif.: 11, 70–71; Joe Seltzer: 188; Copyright © Fred Sons/Uniphoto, Inc.: 123; Tichnor Bros., Boston: 18; Photograph by Larry Witt/Copyright © Dexter Press, Inc.: 4.

Acknowledgments

The publisher wishes to thank the following New York bars and restaurants for their expertise and for graciously allowing photographers to shoot on their premises. Numerals refer to pages on which those sites appear:

Crab House at Chelsea Piers: 84, 89, 92, 102

The Elephant: 47, 52, 96

Fez: 44

Flamingo East: 75, 91

Gramercy Tavern: 115

Harry Cipriani: 86, 133

Indochine: 76

Lei Bar at Niagra: Cover, frontispiece, 20-21, 27, 35, 41, 57, 60, 100-101, 124-25

Mo's Caribbean Bar & Grill: 36, 54, 83, 141

Patria: 43, 72, 95, 110, 119

River Café: 145

Rocking Horse Cafe Mexicano: Back cover, 23, 38, 79, 109, 126

Schaffer City Oyster Bar and Grill: 24, 51, 80, 135

Victor's Cafe 52: 48, 64, 66, 69, 120

Front cover: Bahama Mama. See page 27.
Back cover: Curaçao Cooler. See page 126
Spine: Mango Daiquiri. See page 64.
Frontispiece: Blue Hawaiian. See page 35.

EDITORS: Jeffrey Golick and Nancy Grubb
DESIGNER: Patricia Fabricant
PRODUCTION MANAGER: Richela Fabian
PICTURE EDITOR: Naomi Ben-Shahar
PICTURE RESEARCHER: Scott Hall

10 9 8 7 6 5 4 3 2 1

Library of Congress Cataloging-in-Publication Data

Shelby, Barry.
    Tropical cocktails / text by Barry Shelby : principal photography
  by Kenneth Chen. — 1st ed.
        p.   cm. — (A miniSeries book)
    Includes bibliographical references and indexes.
    ISBN 0-7892-0554-8
    1. Cocktails.   I. Title.   II. Series.
TX951.S544 1999
641.81746dc21

                                              98-43596

ABOUT THE AUTHOR

Barry Shelby was born on the Pacific Coast, a stone's throw from the birthplace of the Mai Tai, and he remembers his first Blue Hawaiian as if it were yesterday. Also the author of Abbeville's *100 Classic Cocktails*, he currently lives in Glasgow with his wife.

Also Available in This Series

Barbie: Four Decades of Fashion
0-7892-0552-1 • 192 pages • $5.95

Cats Up Close
0-7892-0510-6 • 192 pages • $5.95

Elvis: His Life in Pictures
0-7892-0509-2 • 192 pages • $5.95

Horses
0-7892-0526-2 • 192 pages • $5.95

Weddings
0-7892-0524-6 • 192 pages • $5.95

And Try These Tiny Folios™

Hugs and Kisses
0-7892-0361-8 • 288 pages • $11.95

Men Without Ties
0-7892-0382-0 • 288 pages • $11.95

100 Classic Cocktails
0-7892-0426-6 • 288 pages • $11.95